Getting Started In QuickBooks Online 2022

Complete Beginners Guide to QuickBook for Non-Profits, Churches and Small Business

SHELLY G. AARON

Disclaimer Notice:

Please note that the information within this document is for educational and entertainment purposes only. All efforts have been made to present reliable and complete information. No warranties of any kind are implied or declared.

TABLE OF CONTENT:

Introduction

In this book, you'll learn about the first few steps to getting started successfully in QuickBooks. Sometimes, it can be intimidating to start new software; this book is designed to help you feel comfortable and confident to get you off on the right foot.

There are two situations where you're going to get started; the first is;

Part 1; when you start from scratch:
This typically means that you're running a new or relatively new business. In this section, we're going to talk about a few important things;

- How to get around QuickBooks online: here, we'll talk about the three primary ways to navigate the software.
- Then we'll talk about why we should use QuickBooks; here, we'll talk about the power of QuickBooks reports and other benefits

- Then we'll discuss how QuickBooks is built; I'll give you a brief overview of how QuickBooks is designed so you'll understand what you're doing; when you're entering transactions, creating lists and working with other tasks in QuickBooks.

- We'll then review lists; lists are important as they are the building block of what you're going to add to transactions. So, we'll review lists specifically the most important list which is your chart of accounts.

- Then we'll learn how to make your first sale, we'll review how to create an invoice and work with the sales process in QuickBooks.

- And finally we'll connect your bank; we'll set up your bank account and process your first download.

Part two; when you take over from someone else

This could mean that you're taking over from a spouse, it could mean that you're taking over from an accountant or bookkeeper or perhaps a previous employee. It doesn't really matter but this is a very common situation where you take over QuickBooks from someone else.

- We'll also review a couple of key elements to QuickBooks; first, we'll review the chart of accounts as we want to make sure that we know how to work with the account list if that's already there to really make it work for you.

- We'll review the products and services list; once again we'll make sure that it's set up in a way that's going to help your business and find information that's important for you.

- We'll also review the account and settings to make sure that we customize QuickBooks around your business.

- Then we'll learn how to customize invoices, how to make sure that your business is having the right look and feel on your QuickBooks forms.

Now let's get started!

Chapter One: How to Get Around QuickBooks Online

The above image is the QuickBooks starting window and it is known as the dashboard and you can see that on the left hand side, the dashboard is the first thing on the navigation bar. Whatever you have selected on the left will display on the right side of the window.

New Menu

Let's first talk about the new menu; the new menu at the top of the navigation bar is where you will go to enter all of the transactions that you'll enter in QuickBooks. Whether you want to make a sale on an invoice, receive a customer payment, create an estimate for a customer, write a check, create payroll etc. all these can be done from the 'new' menu.

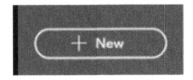

When we click new, it expands into four different columns;

Customers

There's 'customers' and all the transaction listed under it are specific to customer relationships that you have.

Vendors

The 'vendors' deal with suppliers that you may purchase goods and services from (subcontractors etc.).

Employee

'Employees' are those who work for you.

Other

'other' are several different transactions and tasks that you may have to accomplish over a variety of different circumstances in QuickBooks.

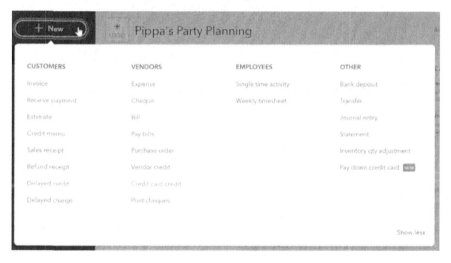

Always use the new menu when it comes to creating any new transactions in QuickBooks.

Navigation Menu

The second option on the left pane is the navigation bar and as we toggle down and hover over any of the title there, QuickBooks will displays the appropriate list items contained within each of them.

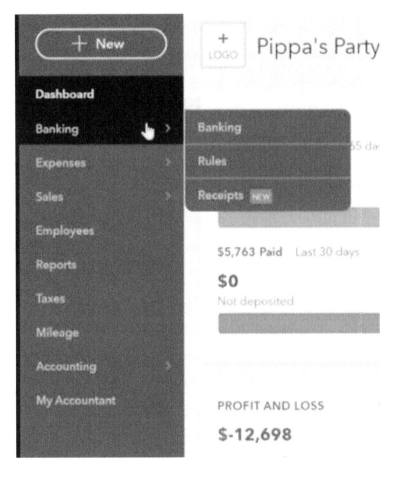

Tabs in the navigation menu;

Banking

In the navigation bar, we'll see 'banking' and this is where we're going to set up our online banking.

Expenses

'Expenses' is where we're going to enter our expense transactions; credit card entries, debit card entries and we'll also find our vendors there.

Sales

Next you'll see 'sales' and this is going to be where we deal with all of our sales transactions in QuickBooks. This is where we're going to create invoices, find our customers and we're going to have an opportunity to review our products and services.

Employees

'Employees' is just about employees and writing payroll checks.

Report

'Reports' is going to be something we'll talk about later but this is where you're going to find a wide variety of preset reports available for you to create at any time to give you information about your business.

Taxes

Next, we'll see 'taxes' and this is where we're going to find sales taxes as well as payroll taxes, both can be found under this menu.

Mileage

Mileage is where you track mileage

Accounting

Accounting is really important for us in this book because we're going to learn about the chart of accounts and how important it is in getting set up the right way and making sure that you get the information out of QuickBooks after you put it in.

My account

Finally, my accountant is where we're going to go to invite our accountant to participate in our accounting.

Always look to the navigation bar when you're dealing with various people in your business whether it's a customer, a vendor, or an employee because that information can be easily found on the navigation bar.

Gear Menu

If we look up in the top right corner, there is a gear menu that is going to contain a variety of things related to your company.

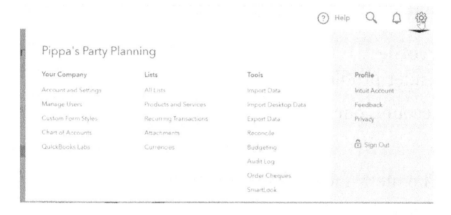

Your Company

This is where you're going to find your account and settings, you'll set up new users here and you'll also find your various forms in your company under custom form styles.

List

You'll also find a wide variety of lists that we will deal with, things like; products and services or transaction lists

Tools

Under tools, we'll be able to do things that are really important for our business, things like; budgeting, reconciling your bank accounts.

Profile

Under profile, we'll see the details about our intuit account, our QuickBooks subscription.

The new menu, navigation menu and the gear menu are the three primary ways to get around; we'll see them in action as we go throughout this book.

Why Use QuickBooks Online?

What are the benefits and why should we use QuickBooks online? And what is QuickBooks online going to do for us?

Let's review some of the importance of QuickBooks online;

1. Tracking business transactions;

Every transaction that goes into your business must be tracked, QuickBooks online helps us do that effectively. Whether you're creating invoices for customers or writing checks to vendors, we want to make sure that we track all business transactions and QuickBooks allows us to do that easily once we learn the first few steps of data entry.

2. Report internally for performance and position of our business

We also want to report internally for the performance of our business and also the position of the business, so we want to have reports to know how profitable we are, we want to know our best customers, we also want to know how much debt we have, our liabilities and our assets. QuickBooks automatically tracks all of this information for us and it's ready whenever we want to create a report; its preset reports that are built as you go. So that's another benefit and power that QuickBooks will offer you.

- Profit and loss

In this specific section, we're going to review the profit and loss report; we'll talk about what it means to create a profit and loss or income statement as we often refer to it

- The balance sheet report

This is going to give you information about the position of your company; you'll know how much debt you have, what your assets are and so on.

- Other financial reports

There are other great reports that will help you find information about your business at any point in time and help you make decisions.

3. Report externally to bodies like the CRA, minister of finance

We also need QuickBooks to help us report externally. When we talk about external vendors and who we might report to, we're talking about things like; the CRA. The Canada revenue agency wants to know our sales taxes, they want to know our payroll taxes and QuickBooks helps us report externally to bodies like them. We might also report to people like; the minister of finance, workers compensation, there's a variety of people and organizations that we're going to report to externally and QuickBooks is going to help us do that efficiently and effectively in our business.

4. Have data to help us make decisions

Finally, we want to have data or information to help us make decisions. We need to know things about our business, we need to know the products and services we're selling, we need to know who our delinquent customers are, we need to know when our accounts payable is out of control and QuickBooks is automatically going to give us all of that information immediately when needed.

These are the reasons we're going to use QuickBooks online and why it's so important that we set it up in a way that's going to be helpful for our business.

QuickBooks Online Report Overview Demo

Let's take a look at some of those powerful reports that we're talking about specifically;

- The profit and loss and
- Balance sheet

To view any reports in QuickBooks, go to the
navigation menu on the left and click on reports.

The above image is the report center; it contains
three tabs full of reports, namely;

Standard

The standard tab at the top will provide us with all
of the preset reports we need when we first get
started in QuickBooks.

First, let's look at our profit and loss report, it's
under favorites. When we open up the profit and
loss report, it is going to tell us the profitability

and the performance of our business over any period of time.

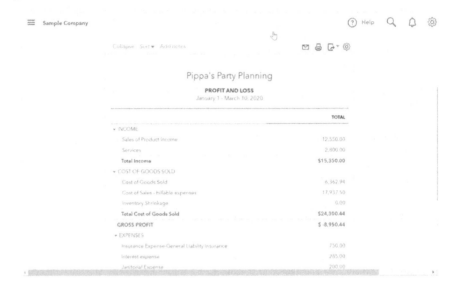

We are mentioning this now because this is what our end goal in QuickBooks is; to make sure that our profit and loss is understandable, readable and that it gives us the information that we need in our business and not what other people need or what they tell us we need but it really gives us the information about how to set up and how to work more effectively in our business.

To look at our balance sheet report, we'll go back to the reports menu and click on balance sheet.

This report is really important to tell us what we own in our company; our assets are things like our machinery and equipment, our accounts receivable or money owed to us. It also gives us information about our liabilities, how much we owe in our company and then finally we have our equity or how much money is left over in the company.

These reports are critical for our business, we're going to create them regularly to help us understand how we're doing, where we're at and making sure that QuickBooks is set up to give us the correct information on these reports is really our end goal. With that in mind, we're now going to jump into our next section.

Chapter Two: How Are QuickBooks Built?

The next step is to understand how QuickBooks is built so that when we go to set everything up, we'll understand what we're setting up and how QuickBooks is going to provide us with the handy reports (the P&L and the balance sheet).

List
First, QuickBooks uses lists as a foundational item to make sure that we're adding the most important people, products and services and accounts to our transactions. So in QuickBooks, we'll set up lists that will store information and they will be the following;

- The customers list and the suppliers list

These are the customers that we're going to sell our products and services to and suppliers or vendors that we're going to purchase products and services from. These can be subcontractors, utilities, retail vendors etc.

- Product and services list

This is what we're going to sell. So if we're a landscape company, we're going to have our landscape services there; maybe we'll have cutting grass, spring cleanup, snow removal etc. These are the types of things we're going to add to our products and services list and we'll review that in detail because it's going to provide us with very important reports in our business to help us understand what we're selling.

- Chart of accounts

We'll also review the chart of accounts. This is the most important list we have in QuickBooks; since every single transaction gets recorded to the chart of accounts, we need to make sure it's set up in a way that works for us and in a way that we understand.

- Helps you complete forms easily and efficiently

The purpose of lists is also to help us complete the forms that we're going to enter in QuickBooks. For example; when we go to create an invoice for a customer, it's really convenient when the customer is already there and we don't have to retype or re-enter or create a new customer from scratch every time we make a sale, so it automates some of that information entry. Things like; the products and services list can attach prices and descriptions, so it makes entering information much faster when the lists are already recorded in QuickBooks.

Transaction Forms
The second thing that we're going to do is that we're going to enter transaction forms. These forms look like paper, when you create an invoice, it looks like an old paper invoice that you might get

in the mail that we might have created 30 years ago. Those transaction forms are critical; we use our list entries to create them, so when we create an invoice, we're going to use the customer list to choose a customer. We're going to use the products and services list to choose the service we're going to provide to them and then we might even use things like the sales tax rate list to make sure we add the right sales tax.

So we're going to use the list to fill out these forms and then when we save the forms, they become our accounting entries. So instead of having to know the debits and credits behind the scenes, the transaction forms do that for us. All you have to do is create your lists, make sure they're set up the right way and then fill out forms for a wide variety of things like; checks, bills, invoices, sales receipts, etc. and then QuickBooks will do the rest for you. So set up the lists, and then add those list information pieces to the transaction forms to do the accounting.

Reports

Finally, we get back to the reports. When we enter transactions, QuickBooks is going to automatically enter them and it's going to build the reports with every subsequent transaction that you enter in QuickBooks.

So keep in mind that setting up your list is a great place to start and then when you add transaction forms, the list information is already going to be there and it's going to make it very efficient for you to enter those transactions.

Let's review this in a nice summary diagram format;

The Chart of Accounts

This is the center of your accounting; this is the core part of what is in QuickBooks. So set up the chart of accounts in a way that works for you.

Don't worry if you don't know what the chart of accounts is because when you first get started, QuickBooks automatically creates a chart of accounts for you. So if you're brand new to business and you don't know what to use, QuickBooks is going to automatically create the chart of accounts for you. As you learn more about your business, you'll be able to edit the chart of accounts to work for you, maybe customize it around your needs.

Everything in QuickBooks is going to flow through the chart of accounts; this means all of these transaction types; invoices, receipts, checks, purchase orders, loan payments, more invoices, deposits and the list goes on and on.

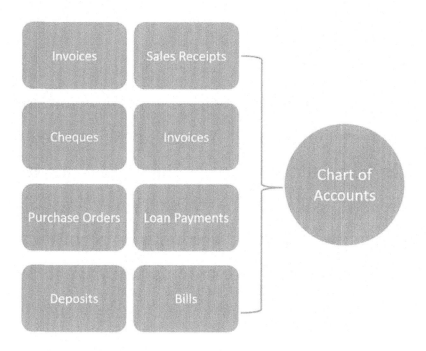

All these transactions are going to flow through the chart of accounts and will eventually give us our accounting reports.

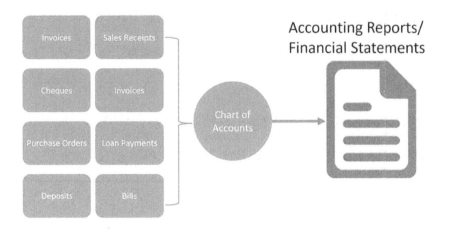

So that's a brief overview of essentially what you'll be doing in QuickBooks. You enter the information on the left; QuickBooks uses the chart of accounts to record all those transactions and then subsequently all the accounting reports and financial statements are automatically created for you.

Enable and Setup Sales Tax

The first list that we're going to cover is the sales tax rate list. It's important to set up your sales taxes correctly so that you can make sure that your sales taxes are being tracked and that we can automate as much as we can by adding sales tax rates to your products and services and in some cases customers. So we always set up the sales tax rates first! Let's go ahead and do that in QuickBooks;

To get started with creating sales taxes in your business; from the dashboard on the left hand side, you'll see the taxes link under the navigation bar, click on it and QuickBooks will start a step-by-step process for creating sales tax.

We'll click on 'set up sales tax' and then we choose the province or territory where we're located.

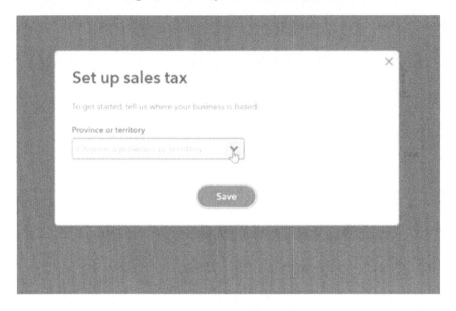

In this example, let's choose Ontario. In Ontario, we only have the HST so QuickBooks will only set up HST because that's the only required sales tax in that province. However if you're based in another province, it will walk you through both the GST and your PST or perhaps QST if you're based in Quebec. Let's click Ontario and then click save and now QuickBooks gives us the option to add information about our specific business situation.

Tell us how you currently handle this tax and we'll do the rest.

Agency
Canada Revenue Agency

Start of tax period

January ⌄

Filing frequency

Quarterly ⌄

Reporting method
◉ Accrual
○ Cash

GST/HST number

So we can add the start of the tax period and the filing frequency which will be based upon the information you receive from the CRA and then we can add the GST/HST number and this number is critical because it is going to display on your sales forms. So make sure you add it at every period where you get the option to add the GST/HST number and that will make sure that you've got the right information displaying on your sales forms for your customers as that is required from the CRA. So we'll leave ours empty for now which is fine and then click next and then click got it and that's all that's required to set up your HST or your GST if you're in Alberta.

Now you can add sales tax to your transactions, and record your sales tax
payments in QuickBooks.
Visit the sales tax page whenever you want to view your history, run reports, or
track payments.

Now let's assume that we're in a different province and we need to add some sales taxes. From the taxes page, click manage sales tax on the top right corner of the screen and once it opens, we can see that we've got a dashboard of what is happening with your current tax.

We're a brand new company so we haven't got anything added yet. I want to show you something here though; click 'add tax' on the top right corner and then QuickBooks will now let you choose 'start tracking tax in a new province', So click add

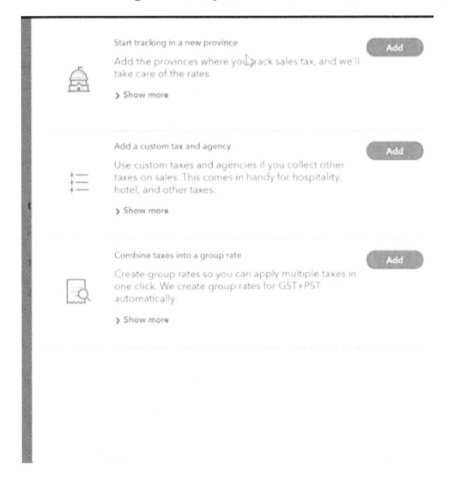

Let's suppose that we are also making sales in Manitoba, so we'll choose Manitoba. We'll end by choosing when our next period starts, let's say March and for filing frequency, let's select monthly. Remember that this will be based upon the information from your agency and then we can add our RST number if required and then we simply click add.

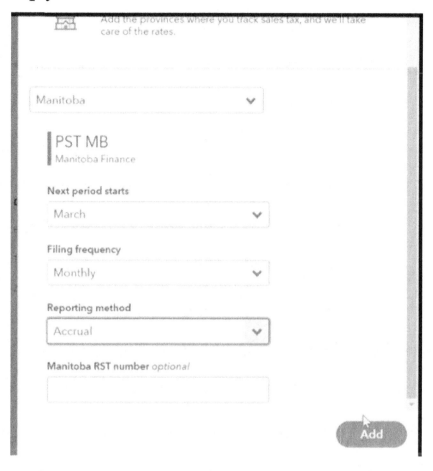

Now we'll have the option to add both our HST as well as any provincial sales taxes related to Manitoba.

So we click done and this now gives us two agencies our Canada revenue agency as well as Manitoba finance.

We want to make sure we do this in advance of creating customers and accounts or modifying our accounts because we can take this sales tax rates and attach them as needed and that will help us automate some of the work down the road. That's why it's step number one on your setup.

If you've already been using QuickBooks or you're just taking over from someone else, this will typically be set up for you so you can leave this as it is and you can add it to accounts and customers whenever necessary.

Adding List Information and Chart of Accounts Setup Demo

The next step in getting set up correctly is adding list information. We reviewed the importance of lists and how they form a foundation of the information that we're going to enter in QuickBooks. We're going to review the chart of accounts in detail; we'll also add a few other list items like; customers and products & services.

Let's get started by looking at our chart of accounts, what it means for us and how to set up accounts;

First we're going to review the chart of accounts;

From the left hand navigation bar, hover over accounting and then click chart of accounts.

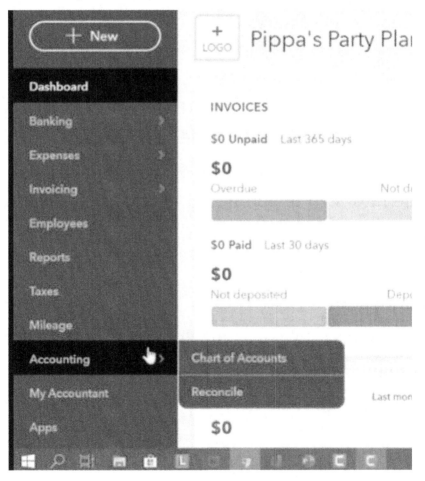

Once you click on it, you'll see that there are two tabs at the top; there's the chart of accounts and reconcile.

In this book, we're only going to talk about the chart of accounts. We're going to click 'see your chart of accounts' and QuickBooks displays the chart of accounts for us.

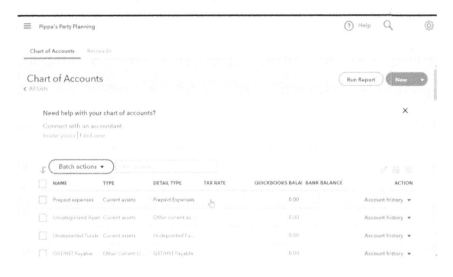

Now a few things that we want to review here is; how the window looks for us.

Name

On the left hand side, you'll notice that there is 'name' under branch actions and that is going to be the name of our account.

Type

The 'type' is going to be the type of account; each account has a different type based on the different category that it is and which report it goes to. At the top of the type of accounts is going to be your asset accounts or your balance sheet account, so that's where we're going to find our chequing account our savings account etc.

Detail type

The other columns 'detail type' is not important so don't worry about that.

Tax rate

The 'tax rate' is when we add a tax to a specific account to automate it, you'll see it displaying there.

The other accounts are the balances at any given time in QuickBooks and what your actual bank balance is.

We can customize this list a little bit to make it easier to look at. To do this, click on the lower gear icon and we can deselect the ones we don't want to see.

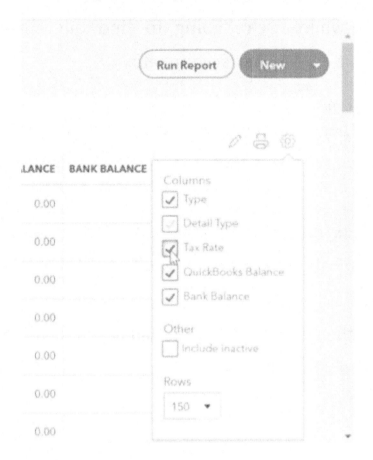

Let's suppose that we don't want to see the detail type and the tax rate columns, we can deselect them and then press the gear icon again and that now provides us with an easier to look and easier to understand chart of accounts.

Now let's add our first account; remember we don't have a bank account, we've just set up QuickBooks. To add a new account, click the new button at the right side and we're going to start by adding an account.

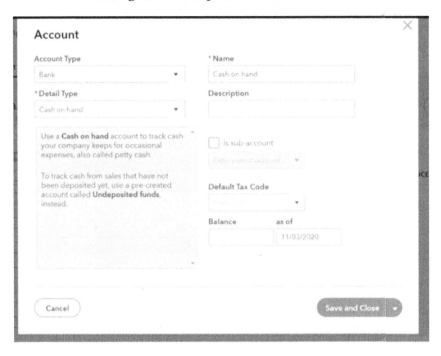

There are only a few key pieces of information you need here, the number one is the account type. When you can click on the drop down of account type, you can see the various types of account. It's broken down into the accounts that are understandable for you as a small business user.

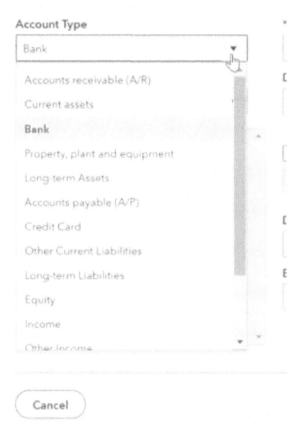

We're going to start by adding our bank account so we'll choose bank. Now, the 'detail type' will give us a little bit more information on the account; a more detail aspect of the account.

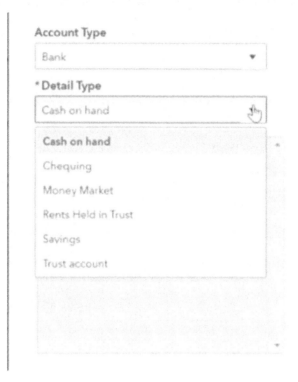

So if this is a chequing account, we'll just choose checking from the drop down options.

After choosing the detail type, let's give a name to our account. Let's suppose that we'll call this 'city credit union chequing'.

Account

Account Type

Bank ▼

* Detail Type

Chequing ▼

Use **Chequing** accounts to track all your
chequing activity, including debit card
transactions.

Each chequing account your company
has at a bank or other financial institution
should have its own Chequing type
account in QuickBooks Online Essentials.

* Name

City Credit Union Chequing

Description

☐ Is sub-account

Enter parent account ▼

Default Tax Code

▼

Balance   as of

11/03/2020

(Cancel)   (Save and Close ▼)

This gives us a name and that will be familiar. Choose a meaningful name for you, so that you'll understand what it is.

That's all we need to do to add a bank account. We don't need to add a balance or anything like that; we'll add that in another way. We don't need to worry about the tax code in this case because there's no tax on our bank account. We're going to save the tax codes and tax rates for our expense accounts. We can now click save and close but in our case, we're going to click on the drop down and select save and new as we'll be creating a couple more accounts.

Expense Account

Now we're going to create an expense account which is going to be the most commonly used type of account in our businesses. We all have a lot more expenses than we want but we need to make sure they're getting tracked properly.

So click on the account type, scroll down and choose expenses. Let's suppose you want to set up an account for marketing, we'll choose the expenses type in the detail type. If you don't see something that suits you, just take your best guess. We'll just select advertising and promotional.

Account

Account Type

Expenses ▼

* Detail Type

Advertising/Promotional ▼

The next thing is to enter the name and we're going to enter a name that's going to work for us. Let's enter 'marketing' as the name.

And then finally, this is an expense account so whenever we incur expenses in Canada, there's always a tax code so we're going to always add a tax code when we can. In this case, we're going to select HST Ontario and that means that every time we get a bill or make an expense transaction to the marketing account, it's always going to add the taxes and we want that to happen because it automates it for us which makes it faster and it makes sure we're capturing everything for sales taxes.

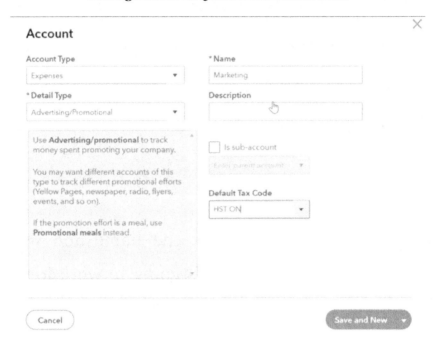

You can repeat this process for creating any account that you would like, it's a good idea to review the accounts that are there because there's going to be lots of great accounts already set up for you but if you need additional accounts, go in and add accounts as needed. We'll click save and close and that adds the account to our chart of accounts.

Now you'll see that our account at the top under 'name' is going to be our 'city credit union chequing'.

Adding a Customer

Let's add a customer; a customer is anyone we're going to make sales to, whether it's someone who comes into our retail location if we have one or someone we're sending invoices to, they're all considered customers.

To add a new customer, we'll hover over invoicing on the left-hand navigation bar.

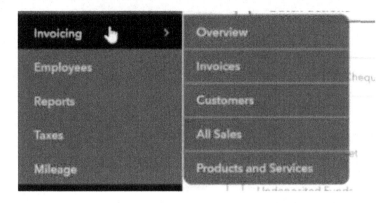

Under invoicing or it may be labeled sales depending on what QuickBooks set up for you, we're going to select customers and you'll see that it'll asks you for your first customers.

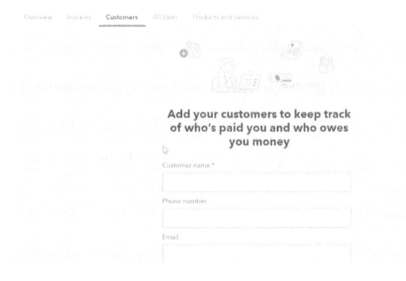

You'll add your very first customer on the 'customer name'; we can add their email and phone number. Then we can click the 'add customer' button and that will start off the customer list.

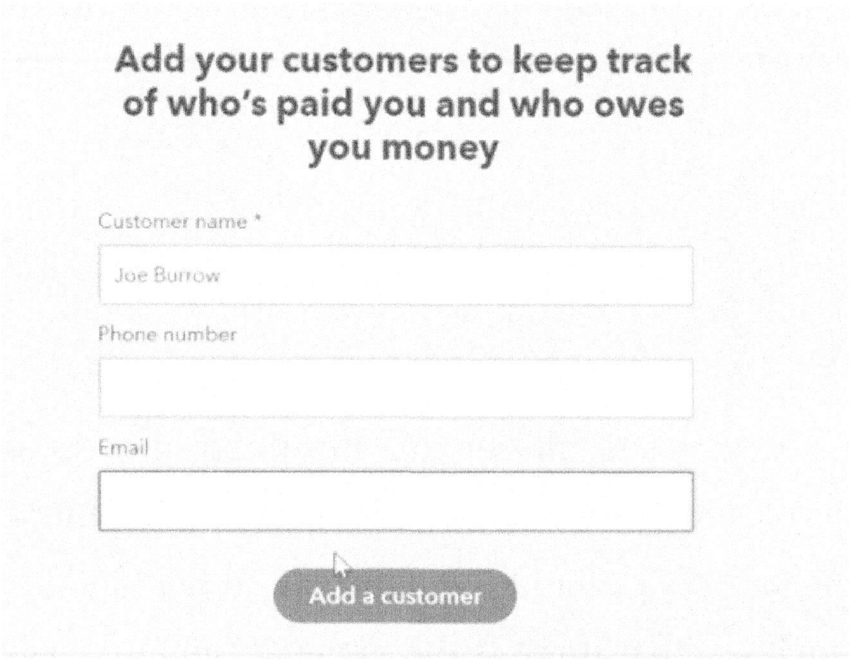

Add your customers to keep track of who's paid you and who owes you money

Customer name *

Joe Burrow

Phone number

Email

Add a customer

If you'd like to add a customer after that first one, you can click on the new customer button in the top right and you'll now see that there's additional information that you can enter.

We're going to fill out this form and once we do that, QuickBooks will add the second customer to the list. We can add the information field by field, you'll see that there is the name at the top, you've got the company name if that's required, you also have a 'display name as', so you can actually choose how your customer name displays on the customer list. I recommend that you choose a naming convention and stick with that because that will help you avoid duplicates and make your customer list easy to read. Add the billing address at the bottom and this is going to be your contact information, and then you can add information such as; email, phone etc.

I recommend adding an email here because if you'd like to email invoices to your customers, it goes a lot faster and is more efficient if the email is already in the customer record.

After adding all of our contact information including the name, address and email, you'll also notice that there are several tabs in the lower half of the window starting with; address, notes etc. let's quickly review a few things in there;

When you click on notes, you can keep any detailed notes on the customer. The customer will never see this because it is an internal thing for you.

We can click on tax info and as mentioned before let's suppose that your client or customer had a specific tax code, they can click the 'assign default tax code' option and they can add a specific tax code. That's why we set up sales tax rates before we set up anything else.

We can click on payment and billing and here we can add terms, preferred payment method and details like that

And if we want to send invoices in different languages, we could do that by clicking on the language.

We can also add any attachments that we have for the customer.

Use the customer setup window to whatever extent is important for your business. This is how we create a customer.

Adding Product and Services

After adding our first customer, we now want to go and add a product or service. This is important because we can track the detailed sales of each of our services in QuickBooks. We want to add product and services to the list so it makes it easy for us to add them to sales transactions at a later time. To add product and services; from the invoicing or sales window, you'll see across the top that there are several options, click products and services.

From the products and services list, click new at the right corner of your screen to add a new service.

You'll see that there are three types; non-inventory, service and bundle.

Let's click on service. In the service, we'll enter the name of our service; we're a party planning company so we're going to enter party planning as our service.

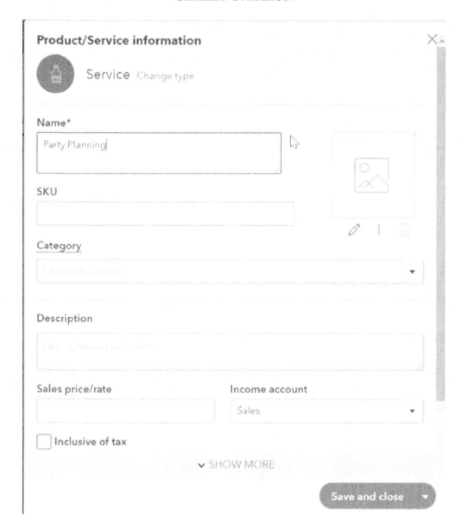

You'll notice that there are a couple of fields there that are optional; we will leave the SKU and category but we'll add a description. The description is going to be important because it's going to display on the customer invoice. So whatever you want to display, make sure you enter it on description. On that note, you don't have to enter a description; you can add the description as you go on a customer invoice. If the description is customized for each sale, I recommend doing it on the sales form itself.

Next we'll enter our sales price. Once again, you can leave this blank or you can add a sales price if it's going to be consistent.

Next you'll see the income account; this is the most important part of this setup. We want to make sure that we track this service to the right income account; this is going to be reflected in our company sales so enter the account you're tracking your sales to. Fortunately, QuickBooks chooses a 'sales' account if you don't have another one that you're going to use and that's recommended because it will make sure that everything gets tracked to the right place on our profit and loss report.

Finally, we'll make sure that we add our tax and that makes sure that every time we sell this service of party planning, we'll make sure that we have our sales tax added to the invoice each time.

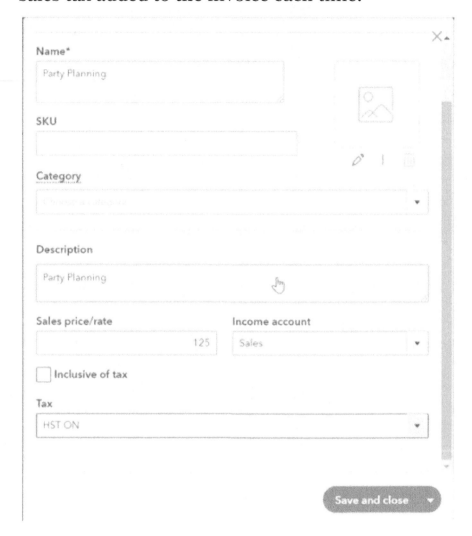

That's all that's required to set up a service.

A few recommended things about services; it's a good idea to set one up for each service that you have. Sometimes people use one umbrella service but they don't get the powerful reporting that QuickBooks offers, so I recommend setting up one service item in QuickBooks for each service that you sell in your business.

Finally we'll click save and close and that adds our first service.

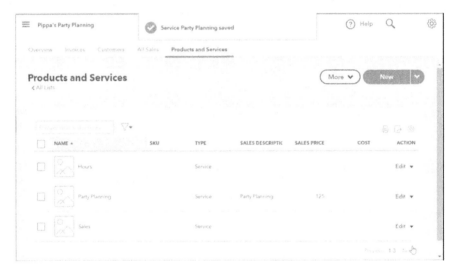

Chapter Three: Make Your First Sales in QuickBooks Online

We're going to talk about making your first sale in QuickBooks. There are three different steps that we're going to use when we create an invoice for a customer;

Invoice workflow in QuickBooks
The workflow goes like this; when a customer promises to pay later, you're going to create an invoice because they're going to pay you at a later time and we're going to track that to what we call our 'accounts receivable' a common term in small business where the customer promises to pay later.

- Invoice

We're going to create an invoice as step number one in the workflow.

- Receive a payment

When the invoice finally gets paid later on, we're going to then receive a payment from the customer and we're going to track that payment to what we call undeposited funds, we'll talk more about that when we get to that step.

- Deposit

Finally, like every dollar that comes into your business, it's going to be deposited at some point.

Invoice Workflow in QuickBooks – Money In

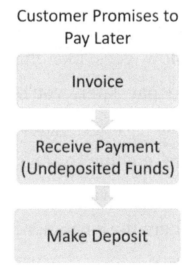

Customer Promises to
Pay Later

Invoice

Receive Payment
(Undeposited Funds)

Make Deposit

Those are the three steps to take when a customer is going to pay later on.

Let's review each of these steps in QuickBooks and see how we follow that from invoice to deposit.

To get started making sales, we're going to click on the new menu in the top left and then we're going to click invoice which is the first option in the customers section.

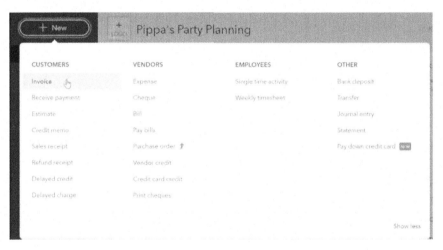

This is the next step in setting up your sales tax. Since we didn't add the business number to begin with, we're going to add that here so that it'll now add to our sales form.

Add sales tax to your invoices   ✕

Share a bit of info to get started

What's your GST business account number (BN)?

> |

What's your PST (MB) business account number (BN)?

>

Save

This is a second reminder to add your GST or HST number and your

PST if you haven't done it already. So we'll enter the information in the business account space and we'll click save. We'll just skip the following page for now we'll talk about that later on.

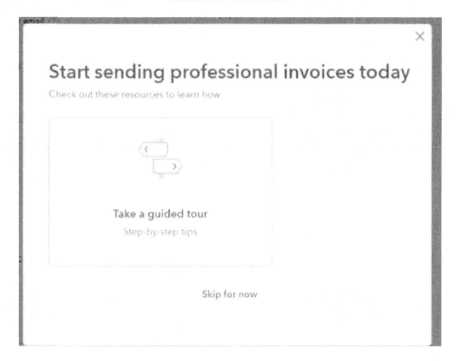

You'll see the invoice form in front of you and it is similar to a paper form that you might fill out in your business.

We're going to focus on four things and we've talked a little bit about that in our transaction form review. We're going to focus on;

- Entering our customer
- The date of the transaction or the when
- We're going to talk about the product or service which is what are we selling to the customers
- And then finally we'll talk about the cost

So we're going to start by entering our customer, the customer column is at the top left corner. Click the drop down menu and choose 'jones wedding'.

And then we're going to add our date and then we'll add our product and service. We have a very simple list right now, so we're going to choose party planning.

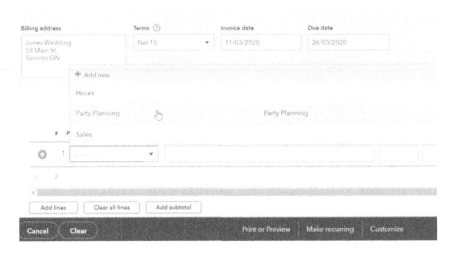

Let's suppose that the quantity is going to be 30 hours at 125 dollars per hour and you'll notice that since we added our sales tax to our party planning service, it automatically calculated for us and that's all we have to do to complete our first invoice.

Let me repeat the process again; we choose our customer, we enter the date of the transaction, we add what we're selling to the customer under product and service and then we'll automatically have the rest calculated because of how the service is set up.

There are a couple of options that you have as well; if you want to proceed, you can actually add more description if you want to and you can customize the invoice number to whatever works for you. That's all that's required here.

Lastly, if we want to save or print or even send it, we can click the down arrow on the 'save and send' button and we can choose 'save and close" and that will save it and close it or we can click 'save and send' and that will give us a preview of the invoice.

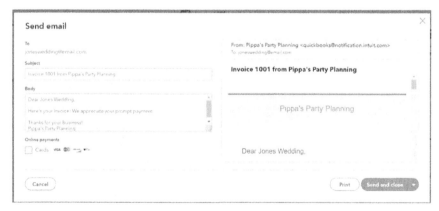

Here we can see the invoice and how it's going to be sent to our customer and they will have it immediately after opening it up in their email.

So whatever works for your business whether it's printing and mailing or emailing, whichever one that works for you, QuickBooks can handle.

Click on save and close and that adds our first invoice.

Receive Customer Payment

The second step in the workflow is to receive the customer payment. In this case, we'll go back and click new and we're going to click on receive payment under invoice and then we're going to fill out this form below.

We're going to choose the customer first, we'll still choose jones wedding and once we do that, you'll see that we have an outstanding invoice.

Let's change the payment date, let's suppose that we received this payment in the future and we'll see that the payment type is a cheque.

The next thing is to enter the reference number. It's a good idea that when you're receiving a check that you enter the reference number or the check number because that's a trackable field especially if we want to look up the history of payments, we can look for the reference number.

After putting the reference number, we're going to select where to deposit this payment. We'll deposit this payment to our undeposited funds account. To do this, click on the deposit to drop down and select that option.

Let me explain why we'll deposit to undeposited funds briefly; *in your business, whenever you receive a check in the mail, you typically don't stand up and go to the bank to deposit that. Generally, you put the cheque somewhere for safekeeping whether that's in your bank book or maybe it's in a folder or whatever it might be but you're going to save that until your next trip to the bank. Now that's what we're doing when we deposit to undeposited funds, we're telling QuickBooks to save this payment in this specific account (money that's waiting to be deposited) and then when we go to the bank, we'll take all the payments that are in that undeposited funds account or all of them that are in our bank book and we'll deposit them all at once.*

So this is mimicking or duplicating what you're actually doing in your business, this is going to be valuable for tracking the payments that you receive and it will also help make sure that all your deposits in QuickBooks match exactly to the deposits in your bank because if you're receiving 5 checks today and you go to the bank once, you're going to only have only one deposit of those five checks.

So you should make sure that you go to the undeposited funds each time and then QuickBooks will make sure that you deposit all of them correctly.

Now we're going to tell QuickBooks that we received this payment. To do that; if they've paid in full, you'll select the invoice in the bottom half of the window and QuickBooks will automatically add the payment and then we can click save and close and that will add the payment and put it into our undeposited funds account.

Making Deposit

The final step is to go to the bank and make the deposit. When we do that, we're going to click the new menu again and we're going to select bank deposit under 'other'.

We only have one payment there but if you had multiple payments, you could select the payments you want to include. Let's say we went to the bank on Monday which is a couple of days after we received the payment. So click on the date and input the date you deposited.

Now, we'll select each payment that's listed under 'select the payments included in this deposit' and QuickBooks will now deposit them into our city credit union chequing.

These are the three critical steps for making your first sale, receiving the payment and then entering the bank deposit. I encourage you to do that right away, when you first get started, create your first sale, get paid for it and then follow those steps to make sure that the payments are deposited into the bank correctly.

So finally we'll click save and close at the bottom and that money gets deposited into the bank.

Just to review what we just did, when we go to accounting in the navigation bar and click on chart of account, we can see that our credit union has 4237.50 in it.

So we've deposited that money and it's now displaying in our bank account. We know that we've done each of the steps correctly and it concludes with the money being deposited into our bank.

Chapter Four: Introduction to QuickBooks Online Banking

We're going to switch gears to our online banking. In this section, we're going to learn why we should use online banking and the first few steps to getting started. This is going to help you automate a lot of the work that you're going to do in QuickBooks and make getting started a lot easier than it ever has been before.

Why Use Online Banking?

First why should we use online banking? This is a good question that we all ask ourselves when we first get started in QuickBooks.

1. It automates your data entry

This means that by connecting your bank account to QuickBooks, it will automatically download transactions into QuickBooks. So instead of you having to enter them from scratch, you simply look at them, review them, edit them if necessary and then add them immediately to QuickBooks. So this takes away a lot of that time consuming data entry.

2. It also helps you stay up to date

One of the biggest problems with bookkeeping in small businesses is that we get busy with everything else that we have to do in running our business; making sales, making sure our team is going where they need to go and we often forget about bookkeeping. When we sign up for online banking and we download it into QuickBooks, it makes sure that our data is always up to date and that our books are accurate.

3. Accurate data entry

Instead of you having to enter things from scratch, QuickBooks actually downloads the actual data. So it's very accurate and it removes any human error that we're prone to do when entering our transactions from scratch.

4. It automates our account reconciliation

One of the most difficult and challenging things that we've experienced in small business bookkeeping is reconciling our bank. This process requires reviewing every single transaction in QuickBooks and making sure it's exactly as it is on our bank statement. When we do the online banking on a regular basis, it auto reconciles those things so when you get to the end of the month as long as you've entered everything from your bank, your bank reconciliation will be done for you automatically. If you've never done bank reconciliation, you might not appreciate that but once you do, you'll understand the great benefit that comes from online banking as it relates to the account reconciliation.

Connecting For the First Time

Let's take a little bit more of a detailed look at online banking. **Connecting for the first time;**

When you go into QuickBooks and you connect for the first time, QuickBooks will take you to this window below and you're going to search for your bank or you can click on one of the common banks that that are listed there.

Connecting for the first time

You can click on any one of those banks listed or search for your bank and the next window will ask you for your sign-in information. So you're going to log into QuickBooks, log into your online banking and you're going to connect the two.

When you log in for the first time, QuickBooks will ask you to connect your bank and ask you which account you want to attach it to in QuickBooks. So you can do this for chequing accounts, savings accounts, other accounts at banks and any credit card account and I recommend you do all of them specifically for the bank account and if you're going to be doing it for credit card account, make sure that it's with a business credit card and not a personal one because it's going to download all the transactions.

Your First Download

When you first get started in QuickBooks, it's not going to know how you tend to work in your bank.

- Download recent transactions

What we're going to do for the first time is we're going to download the transactions to QuickBooks and you can choose the date range that works for you. If you're just getting started in your business, you might not have a long date range but if you're taking over from someone else, you might have a longer date range that you want to download.

- Transactions will start as uncategorized expenses or income

After downloading recent transactions, it's going to start everything off as an uncategorized income transaction or an uncategorized expense. So it's either going to be money into our business as income or money out as expenses and each one of those will have a label and you'll be able to edit each of the transactions and tell QuickBooks how to categorize them; the account you want to track them to and the sales tax rate that is applicable.

So that's how we're going to first get started.

Categorize Your First Online Banking Download Demo

The great thing is, once you get started, QuickBooks is going to learn how you work and it will begin to automatically categorize the transactions for you. Let's take a look at what this means for our first banking download;

To get started with your first download, click the banking link on the left hand side and then click banking from the options. The below image is the online banking window

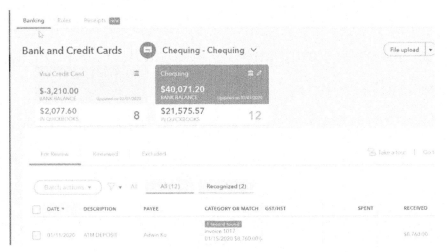

At the top, you'll see three tabs starting with banking and this is where you're going to do almost all of your work. You can get to 'rules' later on where you can establish bank rules that will tell QuickBooks how to handle certain transactions and a fairly new feature where you can take pictures of receipts, we'll talk about that later on.

In this banking page, we're going to deal with the first account which is our chequing account; down at the bottom of the window, you'll see a list of transactions. These transactions are associated with the account that is clicked up and is highlighted in blue, so we're dealing with our chequing account and its transaction is what we see at the bottom.

The number 12 below the blue highlight represents the number of transactions that we need to work on to do our first categorization of our first download. So let's scroll down and look at what is going to be required of us.

In the bottom half of the window, we see three tabs; for review, reviewed and excluded.

The 'for review' tab includes all of the transactions that have not been added to QuickBooks from our banking download which is what we're about to review now. After they're added to QuickBooks, they'll move to the reviewed tab.

Occasionally, we might need to exclude a transaction, when we exclude, it will be added to 'excluded'.

The first thing you're going to do is to look at each of the transactions there and categorize them as needed. The first transaction you'll see is '1 record found' and this is an invoice.

From the left side of your screen, you'll see date and that is going to be the date of the transaction.

The description is going to be the type of transaction it is in your bank and in this case, it says it's a deposit. That's good because we know that this is money coming into our business.

It now shows us the payee and it shows that there's a category or match and it says that there's 1 record found which means that QuickBooks has scanned your file and it has found a deposit that matches that transaction. So if we click on that transaction, we can see that it's an invoice for 1017 for the amount of 8760 and QuickBooks has automatically found the transactions for us.

Add ⦿ Match Not sure?

Record found

Invoice 1017 01/15/2020 $8,760.00 (open balance) Adwin Ko | (Find other records)

BANK DETAIL ATM DEPOSIT ATM DEPOSIT 00003174

| | 01/04/2020 | ATM DEPOSIT | Ho Engineering Co. | | 1 record found Sales Receipt 01/03/2020 $480.00 Ho Engineering Compa |

| | 01/04/2020 | ATM DEPOSIT Ko | | Uncategorized Inco... |

Now that might not always happen, we might need to do a little bit of work but generally speaking, when there's deposits and they match amounts in QuickBooks it's automatically going to do the work for us.

So now we scroll over to the right and we simply click match and that gets added to QuickBooks immediately. So that's our first transaction down.

The next transaction also says that there's a record found in our sales receipt, so we can click match on that as well and it gets added to QuickBooks.

The third one is going to require a little bit more work; remember that if you want to remove columns, you can always click the gear icon and you can remove the columns. So let's remove some columns to make it easier to understand.

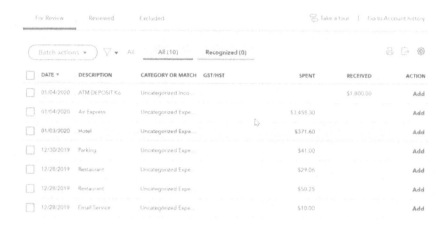

In this example, we're going to click on the transaction which is an ATM deposit and it's for $1800 and we need to make sure we find it in QuickBooks because we don't want to just add it if there's something that it matches already.

In this example, instead of it matching automatically, we're going to select 'find match' next to Add and this is going to let us look at the outstanding invoices and see if they match this deposit that we've just made.

Once we click the find match, QuickBooks opens up the window below and we can look at the transactions from there.

If you scroll down the page, you'll see that QuickBooks actually found two transactions; one is from Kathy's consulting for $1,600 and the other is from hazel Robinson for $200 and those two transactions make up the one deposit.

So we know that we have the right deposit amount and we know that the payment is being applied against these invoices. Sometimes, deposits are going to be made up of multiple payments from customers just like I showed you in the previous window for receiving customer payments that is the same thing we see on this window.

Once we've added the deposit, we can click save and that'll add the deposit to our QuickBooks.

The rest of the transactions are going to require a little bit more work because it has uncategorized expense for each the transaction.

DATE ▾	DESCRIPTION	CATEGORY OR MATCH	GST/HST	SPENT	RECEIVED	ACTION
01/04/2020	Air Express	Uncategorized Expe...		$3,458.30		Add
01/03/2020	Hotel	Uncategorized Expe...		$371.60		Add
12/30/2019	Parking	Uncategorized Expe...		$41.00		Add
12/28/2019	Restaurant	Uncategorized Expe...		$29.06		Add
12/28/2019	Restaurant	Uncategorized Expe...		$50.25		Add
12/28/2019	Email Service	Uncategorized Expe...		$10.00		Add
12/28/2019	IT Support Center	Uncategorized Expe...		$100.00		Add

We're going to start with the restaurant transaction and I'm going to show you what QuickBooks will do when we click on it. So let's click on the restaurant transaction. In the category, we'll enter 'meals and entertainment' then we're going to add the sales tax code and we're going to choose HST. QuickBooks adds a question asking us if we'd like to automate that, so we'll say yes. Once we add our first transaction, we'll click add and QuickBooks recognizes the other descriptions labeled restaurant and it automatically adds meals and entertainment to each of the transaction and adds the appropriate sales tax.

Banking	Rules	Receipts NEW

	DATE ▼	DESCRIPTION	CATEGORY OR MATCH	GST/HST	SPENT	RECEIVED
☐	01/04/2020	Air Express	Uncategorized Expe...		$3,458.30	
☐	01/03/2020	Hotel	Uncategorized Expe...		$371.60	
☐	12/30/2019	Parking	Uncategorized Expe...		$41.00	
☐	12/28/2019	Restaurant	Meals and entertain...	HST ON (Purchases)	$50.25	
☐	12/28/2019	Email Service	Uncategorized Expe...		$10.00	
☐	12/28/2019	IT Support Center	Uncategorized Expe...		$100.00	
☐	12/27/2019	Supply Depot	Uncategorized Expe...		$200.75	
☐	12/27/2019	Restaurant	Meals and entertain...	HST ON (Purchases)	$37.65	

Batch actions ▼   All   All (9)   Recognized (2)

1-8 of 8

So QuickBooks is going to learn your tendencies and how you're going to make expenses in QuickBooks. Instead of having to go back and enter each of the transaction, we can click 'add' on each of the transaction and it adds the transaction to QuickBooks.

You'll see that we've got just a couple transactions left to complete our first download.

	DATE ▾	DESCRIPTION	CATEGORY OR MATCH	GST/HST	SPENT	RECEIVED	ACTION
☐	01/04/2020	Air Express	Uncategorized Expe...		$3,458.30		Add
☐	01/03/2020	Hotel	Uncategorized Expe...		$371.60		Add
☐	12/30/2019	Parking	Uncategorized Expe...		$41.00		Add
☐	12/28/2019	Email Service	Uncategorized Expe...		$10.00		Add
☐	12/28/2019	IT Support Center	Uncategorized Expe...		$100.00		Add
☐	12/27/2019	Supply Depot	Uncategorized Expe...		$200.75		Add

1-6 of 6

Next we're going to click on the 'air express' and in the category, we're going to enter travel and we'll add our sales tax code and then click add and it'll add that transaction to QuickBooks.

Repeat the same process for each of the remaining transaction till you complete it.

You'll notice that when we add a transaction and it already has other similar transactions there; it will highlight it in green.

Another thing to note is that we're not adding suppliers when we open a transaction but we can add suppliers as an option. When we add supplier to a transaction, enter the category, tax code and click save, it gives a bit more detail rather than just knowing the category and sales tax, it also adds the supplier name and that can be helpful.

Once we're done with all the transactions, it means that we've added all our first transactions. Now our first download is complete and we have no further transactions to add.

For the first download, Go through the activity of making sure that you categorize everything either as money in like we did for the deposits or money out and make sure that the right account is attached with the right sales tax code and that's all that's required for your first download.

From then on, your downloads will become easier and easier as QuickBooks learns how you do your accounting, it will begin to make suggestions and it will begin to automatically categorize the items for you and that's why I recommend you do this immediately you first get started in QuickBooks so you can start to automate your work and take some of the load off when you're working in QuickBooks.

Chapter Five: Taking Over From Someone Else

We're going to shift gears and talk about part two which is taking over from someone else. This can mean a variety of things for different businesses; it might mean that you're taking over from your spouse; it could be taking over from an accountant or bookkeeper who has provided you with information but now you have to take over, it could be taking over from a former employee, whatever the case is.

Taking over from someone else always requires a little bit of review so that you'll feel comfortable knowing what to do. Everything we've done in starting from scratch is applicable here but now we're going to take that to another level and talk a little bit more about customizing things after you take over from someone else.

Even if you're working in QuickBooks from scratch, this part is going to be very valuable in order to understand how to refine your QuickBooks to help you get a little bit more out of it and make sure that you're categorizing and working with the right accounts and products and services in your business.

QuickBooks Review Checklist

I'm going to take you through a QuickBooks review checklist. If you're just taking over, this is a quick checklist that you can do and I'll teach you how to do each one of these items.

- Review the chart of accounts

Make sure you edit the chart of account to work for you. Even though you're taking over, it might even be your business and you might not have the accounts that you want on it to provide you the information that you need. So I'll make sure you learn how to edit the chart of accounts and customize it.

- Review the product and services list

We want you to review the products and services list making sure that you are recording the things that are important for your business.

- Review account and settings

Then we'll review the account and settings; how to customize QuickBooks features around what you need in your company and sometimes you can even turn features off if they're confusing you or if you've got too much information on your QuickBooks windows.

We can turn some features off if they're not being used in order to make it easier to record and understand what's going on in QuickBooks.

- Customize your forms

And finally we'll look at how to customize your forms. I get this question often from people who are just getting started. Starters often wonder how they'll customize forms to add logo and to do a variety of things that are going to help them customize QuickBooks around their business.

QuickBooks Chart of Accounts Review

First, let's talk about the chart of accounts review.

- It's a good idea to edit accounts in order to make sure that the names match what you need on reports. So if you've got a bunch of names that don't mean anything to you, you can edit the account names to make sure that they work for your understanding of your business.

- We also want to clean up any account that is not being used in order to make accounts inactive. If you've got lots of accounts on the chart of accounts that are not being used and are just cluttering up the account list, we can make them inactive to make it easier to read.

- We can also merge accounts. So if you've got duplicate accounts and you want to just pare that down, you can merge the accounts. This also goes for other things like; if you have duplicate customers or duplicate suppliers, you can merge those items as well. We'll review how to do that on the chart of accounts.

Review the Chart of Accounts Demo

Let's go to QuickBooks to do all the above listed;

Let's get started on the chart of accounts so we're going to click accounting and then choose chart of accounts.

Chart of Accounts   Reconcile

NAME	TYPE ▲	DETAIL TYPE	CURRENCY	TAX RATE	QUICKBOOKS B/ BANK BALANCE		ACTION
☐ Uncategorised A	Current assets	Other curren...	CAD		0.00		Account history ▾
☐ Uncategorized A	Current assets	Other curren...	CAD		0.00		Account history ▾
☐ Undeposited Fur	Current assets	Undeposited ...	CAD		0.00		Account history ▾
☐ Accumulated De	Property, pla...	Accumulate...	CAD		-366.63		Account history ▾
☐ Furniture and Eq	Property, pla...	Furniture an...	CAD		2,750.00		Account history ▾
☐ Leasehold Impro	Property, pla...	Leasehold I...	CAD		0.00		Account history ▾
☐ Vehicles	Property, pla...	Vehicles	CAD		0.00		Account history ▾
☐ Accounts Payable	Accounts pa...	Accounts Pa...	CAD		734.51		Account history ▾
☐ Accounts Payable	Accounts pa...	Accounts Pa...	HKD		0.00		Account history ▾
☐ Visa Credit Card	Credit C...	Credit C...	CAD		2,077.60	-3,210.00	Account history ▾
☐ GST/HST Payable	Other Curre...	GST/HST Pay...	CAD		752.33		Account history ▾

Edit Account

The first cleanup option that we have is to edit accounts. It is a good idea to edit an account that may or may not be telling you what you need. Let's take the chequing account for example, we might have multiple chequing accounts and we might want to edit the name to give us more specific information.

To edit an account, we'll go to the right corner of any account, click the drop down arrow on accounting history and then choose edit.

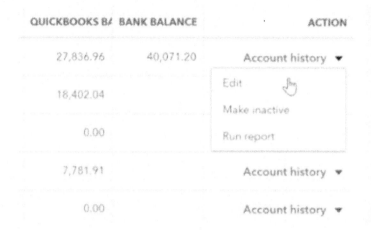

QUICKBOOKS B⟍	BANK BALANCE		ACTION
27,836.96	40,071.20		Account history ▾
18,402.04			Edit
			Make inactive
0.00			Run report
7,781.91			Account history ▾
0.00			Account history ▾

The next window it'll open is one that you're
familiar with.

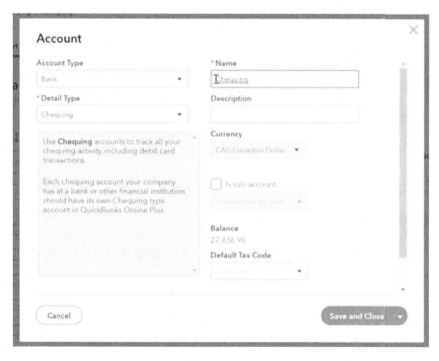

In the window above, we're going to edit the name; we're just going to enter our company business account. So we're going to enter the company name as RBC chequing and that will give us more detail.

You can edit the name on any account but you can't edit the account type and detail type, so we're just concerned about the name and description of the account. We can also add subaccounts if we want.

Once you edit the account, you can click save and close and that'll give us a more specific name on our chart of accounts.

If you want to add additional information to the account, you can also click edit and you can add any additional description or details that are necessary.

Clean Up Account

Let's clean this account so we can make it a bit easier to read. To do that, we're going to click on the gear icon and we're going to unmark the things that are not important for us.

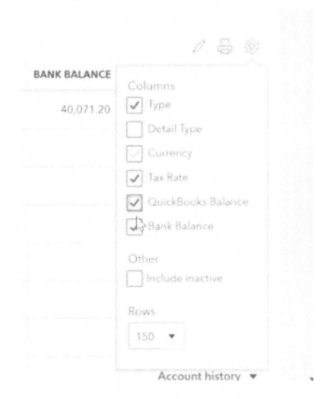

This makes it a bit easier to read.

The next thing is to make accounts inactive. If you see accounts on the chart that are not being used and they don't have any balance or history in them, you're free to go and make them inactive.

Let's suppose that we know we're not going to be doing leasehold improvements, we can click the drop down arrow on the account history of that transaction and we can choose 'make inactive'.

Once we click on make inactive, it'll bring up a prompt asking if we're sure, click on yes and that will make that account inactive and it'll no longer appear on the chart of accounts.

We can do the same thing for other accounts, for example let's suppose that we don't want to be using the 'uncategorized asset' account, we can make it inactive as well using the same method we used earlier.

We can always bring back the accounts we made inactive if we want. To do that, click on the gear icon and you'll see the option to show inactive, Click on the box and that will display all the accounts that are inactive and then from there, you can make them active using the same way we used in making them inactive.

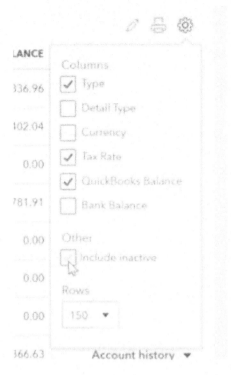

The accounts we make inactive do not get deleted, they're still there but are just inactive and essentially suppressed from your chart of accounts.

Merge Account

Finally, if we want to be able to merge accounts we can do that as well. To do that, let's scroll down to the bottom of the chart of accounts and go to our expenses section and merge two accounts that are similar from there. Under expenses, we'll go down to our travel section

Here we have travel expense and travel. Let's suppose that we want to merge travel expense into travel. To do that, we're going to remove the account that we want to merge. Click on the travel expenses drop down menu on account history and click on edit. We're simply going to change the name of this account (travel expenses) to the exact same name as the other account (travel) and in doing that, QuickBooks will then allow us to merge those accounts. After editing the name, click on save and close, it tells us that name is already being used and asks if we would you like to merge the two.

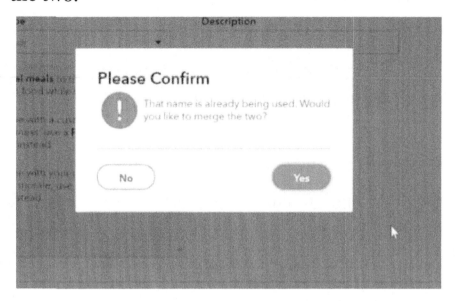

We'll click yes and QuickBooks merges those two accounts.

The important to understand is that this is something you can't undo without doing individual work on transactions. So just be careful when you go to merge accounts, be sure that you want to do it because it's not something you can easily undo.

Let's merge one more time; let's scroll down to the bottom again and go to our expenses, we'll see travel and travel meals and we're going to take the travel meals and we're going to merge it into travel. Simply edit the travel meal and change the name to travel, we'll click save and close and then we've merged those two as well.

Those are the three tools to clean up the chart of accounts and customize it around what you need. Edit the accounts as needed, make accounts that are not being used or have never been used or don't have a balance inactive and then merge any duplicates or any redundant accounts that you don't want to have around so you can get a nice clean chart of accounts and that will then translate nicely to your profit and loss and balance sheet reports. This will make your report easy to read, easy to understand and you'll be able to make decisions more effectively.

Product and Services List

The next element to review is your products and services list. To do this, click on sales on the left pane and then select products and services from the options.

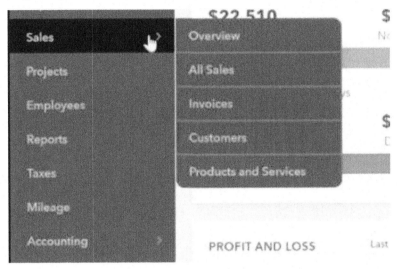

Here, we can also do the similar types of things that we did to our chart of accounts.

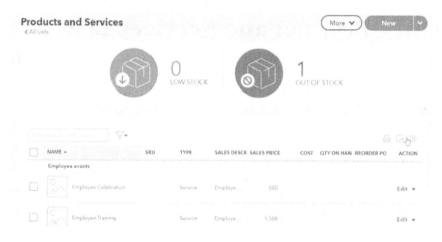

We can edit names; if we want to edit any item, we click on edit on the right corner and we can change the name of the item, we can also change the category; if we're going to be tracking it to a specific income account, make sure they're all going to the account of your choosing.

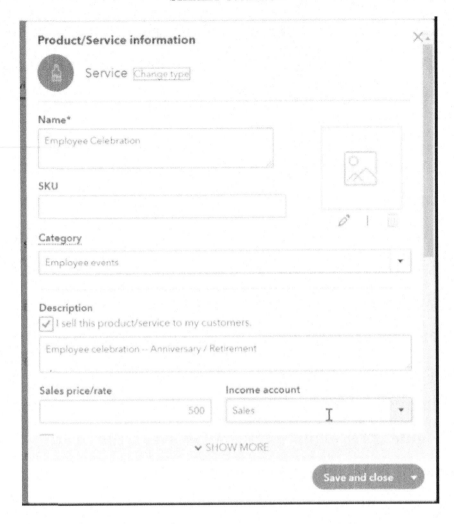

Sometimes we add way too many income accounts and you'll find lots and lots of accounts there, try to get them all pointed at a minimum set of accounts. Ask your accountant if you're unsure of how to do that or ask them for the accounts to use rather and they'll be able to tell you which accounts to use. It's a good idea to keep them in just a few accounts and then your profit and loss report will be much easier to use.

Another thing I recommend doing here is making sure that you have one product or service for every product or service you sell in your business. A good example of this is; let's suppose that you're an engineering firm and you provide 30 different services, in your chart of accounts, you should set up a service for each of those 30 different services whether it's; junior engineering, senior engineering consulting whatever the category might be. Each service you offer you should set up an individual service item for it.

If you set up just one blanket item then you will only have one item displaying on your sales reports and that can be a disadvantage when you're trying to report on your business. So make sure that you have a service item or a product if you're using inventory or other items, make sure that each one is set up individually and that way, you can get a nice report.

Let me show you what we mean by that;

Click on the reports menu on the left pane and scroll down and you'll see that there is an option there for sales and customers.

And under it, we have an item or a report called 'sales by customer detail' click on it.

There we can see that we've got specific sales for each customer which is very valuable. We can also go back to reports and under the same category (sales and customers), we'll see 'sales by product service detail' click on it.

DATE	TRANSACTION TYPE	#	CUSTOMER	MEMO/DESCRIPTION	QTY	SALES PRICE	AMOUNT	BALAN
▾ General services								
▾ Badges								
▾ Name Badges								
03/10/2020	Invoice	1016	Anilkumar Pillai	Name Badges	300.00	3.00	$900.00	900
Total for Name Badges					300.00		$900.00	
Total for Badges					300.00		$900.00	
▾ Services								
03/10/2020	Invoice	1013	Whitehead and Sons	Monthly consulting agreement	8.00	150.00	$1,200.00	1,200
Total for Services					8.00		$1,200.00	
▾ Water Bottles - Generic								
03/10/2020	Invoice	1016	Anilkumar Pillai	Water bottles - generic	300.00	10.00	$3,000.00	3,000
Total for Water Bottles - Generic					300.00		$3,000.00	
Total for General services					608.00		$5,100.00	
TOTAL					608.00		$5,100.00	

Accrual basis Wednesday, March 11, 2020 04:11 PM GMT-05:00

There, we'll be able to see each of the individual items that we have for sale, whether it's a service, a non-inventory, an inventory part, they're all going to be detailed out nicely for us.

This is where we're going to see the advantages of entering each individual item by itself as opposed to group items. So make sure you set up the products and services list in a way that's going to be helpful for you on this report.

If you've got too few items and you're not quite sure of what you're selling, make sure you add items. If you have duplicates, I don't recommend merging the duplicates but you can make items inactive. To make an item inactive in our product and service list, let's go back and select our products and services list, let's suppose that we're no longer doing the 'name badges', we can click the drop down of edit at the right corner and we can choose 'make inactive' and that will make that item inactive and it will no longer display on our products and services list or on sales transactions to be sold.

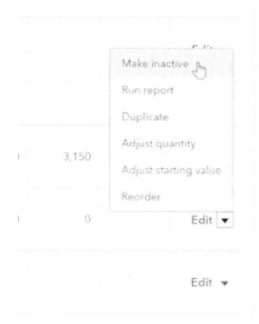

You can also do the same thing to any other item you think you're not making use of. Click the drop down on edit and make them inactive and clean up your products and services list and make it work for your business.

Account and Setting

The last item for review is the account and settings. To access accounts and settings, click the gear icon at the top left corner of the screen and then click account and settings.

The first thing we want to do once the window opens is to go under the company section and edit any details we want.

You can add your company logo; you can change your contact information, your address etc. all those details can be edited here. So make the necessary changes that fit your need. You can click on sales on the left corner of the screen and you can change the sales form content.

If you want to add or remove items that are available on your sales forms you can do that on the sales form category. Simply click that section and then you can choose to add things like; discounts, deposits, custom fields etc.

Settings

Preferred delivery method ⑦   None ▼

☐ Shipping ⑦   Off

Custom fields ⑦   Off

    Name   Internal Public

    Event Rep   ☐

                                  ☐

                                  ☐

☑ Custom transaction numbers ⑦   On

☐ Service date ⑦   Off

☐ Discount ⑦   Off

☐ Deposit ⑦   Off

   Cancel   **Save**

Products and services   Show Product/Service column on sales forms   On

            Show SKU column   Off

You can add everything as you need to. Once you do that, you click save, make sure you save each category so that they're being saved as you go.

You'll see that you can add additional features if necessary things like; progress invoicing, reminders and details like that can be added under the sales section. Depending on your subscription, you may or may not see some of these things. For example; progress invoicing is available in QuickBooks online plus, so you would not see it if you had the essentials version.

Under expenses still on the left corner, we can turn some features off if we're not using them.

Bills and expenses	Show items table on expense and purchase forms	On
	Track expenses and items by customer	Off
	Make expenses and items billable	Off
	Default bill payment terms	
Purchase orders	Use purchase orders	Off
Messages	Default email message sent with purchase orders	

Privacy | Security | Terms of Service

For example, if you click on the bills and expenses section, you might see that you have a lot of details about customers on expenses and you wonder why it is that way. You can disable any feature by deselecting it, if you're not using billable expenses and if you're not tracking your expenses to each customer, you can disable that and it makes your data entry that much faster because you don't have any extra fields on your forms.

119

Feel free to deselect the features you don't need and that will clean up a little bit of clutter on some of the QuickBooks windows. Click on save to make sure you save the change.

Finally if we click on advanced on the left corner, we can edit some important things there.

Accounting	First month of fiscal year	January	
	First month of income tax year	Same as fiscal year	
	Accounting method	Accrual	
	Close the books	Off	
	Default tax rate selection	Exclusive of Tax	
Company type	Tax form	Sole proprietor	
Chart of accounts	Enable account numbers	Off	
Categories	Track classes	Off	
	Track locations	Off	
Automation	Pre-fill forms with previously entered content	On	
	Automatically apply credits	On	
	Automatically invoice unbilled activity	Off	
	Automatically apply bill payments	On	

 If you've been told to use account numbers by your accountant, you can turn on account numbers when you click on 'enable account numbers'. Click on save and that turns on account numbers.

You can also enable features like tracking classes and this is if you want to track different departments or business units in your company.

And if you're not using them and they're turned on, feel free to turn them off and that way you don't have to worry about having too much information on the sales or expense forms.

If you have track classes enabled and you don't need it then you can certainly go in and disable it, click save and that will make sure you clean up the account and settings.

Finally, when you scroll to the bottom, make sure that you change the date format to work for you. If you're using a specific date format you can select it from there as well as a number format and I recommend turning some options there on.

Turn on 'warn if you've got duplicate cheque numbers or bill numbers' and that'll make sure you avoid any duplicate transactions and confusion in your data entry. Click on save and that saves the features.

I recommend going through the account and settings and editing as much information as needed and turn on or off features that work for your business and to make QuickBooks easier to use.

Customizing Sales Forms Demo

The last area of review is customizing sales forms. Let's take a look at how we're going to do that in QuickBooks;

To access your customized forms in QuickBooks, click the gear icon at top left corner and then choose custom form styles under your company.

In this example, we're going to create a new one; you can create a new form for invoices, estimates and sales receipts. We're going to choose invoice.

First, you should name your template, so enter the name you want under the design tab, the name you choose is going to be how you refer to the invoice in QuickBooks and you can choose from different forms if you add multiple customized forms.

You'll see across the top that you've got design, content, emails and payments. Emails and payments are going to be specific to your company. If you're going to be emailing your clients or customers invoices, you can change the language that you use and you can turn on payments.

We're going to focus on design and content here. The design tab lets you choose a few different things; first you can choose a specific template.

You can see that we've got five or six templates, you can choose one and QuickBooks gives you the preview on the right hand side then you can actually choose your logo. You can choose make logo edits and you'll be able to add a new logo from there.

If you want to hide your logo, you can just choose hide logo and then it won't display there for you.

You can change the color by clicking splash on some color. Let's suppose that we want to make this a nice pink, we'll add that color palette there.

INVOICE TO			
Smith Co			
123 Main Street	Invoice 12345		
City, ON K1T 2T1	DATE 01/02/2018 TERMS Net 30		
Business account number	DUE DATE 24/07/2018		
987654321 RT 0001			

ACTIVITY	QTY	RATE	AMOUNT
Item name	2	225 00	450 00
Description of the item			
Item name	1	225 00	225 00
Description of the item			

It's a pleasure doing business with you. Hope ember referrals are appreciated	SUBTOTAL	675 00
	HST @ 10.0%	113 00
	GST @ 5.0%	105 00
	TOTAL	$893 00
	TOTAL DUE	$893.00

Tax summary

RATE	TAX	NET
HST @ 10.0%	90 00	450 00
GST @ 5.0%	11 25	225 00

We can change our font when we choose 'get choosy with fonts' and then you can customize your margins and your printing.

These are the design elements to customizing forms.

More importantly is the content option. When you choose content, there are three different sections; there's the header, the body and the footer. Each one of these sections can be customized according to your needs.

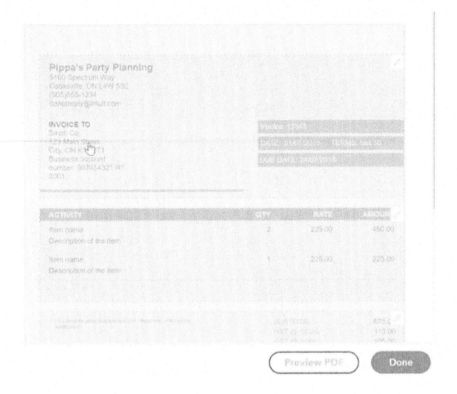

We'll click the header to get started. Once you click the header, you'll see that you can add your business name, phone and email. You can also add your address depending on what you want to display. You can select or deselect things from the template.

As you scroll down, you'll see that you can add the form name, you can change it from invoice to whatever you want. You can add form numbers and other details and then you can add different information in the header to display. Let's suppose we don't want to add terms, due date or our customer number, we can make it very simple and take elements off of the form as well as adding them and once you make any changes you'll see it being reflected in the preview on the right hand side.

Let's click the body of the invoice and we want to include the things that are important to us.

Let's say we don't want our customers to see the product or service name, we just want them to see the description. So we'll deselect the product and services and we'll just choose description. Maybe we don't want to see quantity and rate, we just want to have amount, simply deselect the ones you don't want and select the ones you want.

If we're a service based business, this is often how we'll do things where we'll have a description and then a flat amount for the services we're providing but you can customize in whatever way works for you. You can also reorder the columns by dragging the little round icons up or down to reorder them from left to right.

COLUMNS   EDIT LABELS AND WIDTHS

- [ ] Date
- [ ] Product/Service
  - [ ]
  - [ ] Category
- [x] Description
  - [ ] Include Quantity and Rate
- [ ] Quantity
- [ ] Rate
- [ ] Tax
- [x] Amount

Feel free to go and order them in a way that makes sense for your customers.

Finally, if you'd like to edit the label or the width of the columns, click the edit labels and widths column and you can change the details there.

Finally we'll click on the footer and we'll change any footer information. We'll keep it at tax summary and we'll add any other details as you scroll down.

If you'd like to add payment details and other information, you can certainly add that and QuickBooks will then display it on your form.

Finally to complete this, we'll want to preview this invoice. So we'll click preview PDF and we'll see a simple preview of what the invoice will look like for our customer.

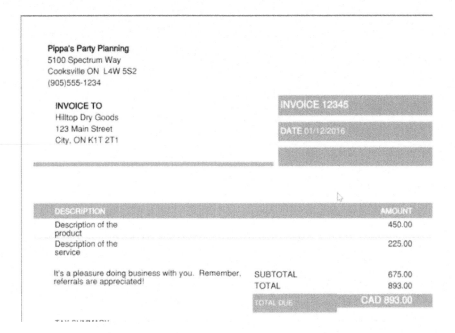

This is an easy way to customize QuickBooks around your business and make it friendlier to read for a customer and hopefully you get paid that much faster. We'll close the preview and we'll click done and we'll save that in QuickBooks.

That completes customizing form styles and that completes our getting started in QuickBooks book.